Warriner's English Grammar and Composition

LIBERTY EDITION

Complete Course